THE NEW FAMILY

Your Child's First Year

By Fairview Health Services
Affiliated with the University of Minnesota

Fairview Press
Minneapolis

Published by Fairview Press, 2450 Riverside Avenue, Minneapolis, Minnesota 55454. Fairview Press is a division of Fairview Health Services, a community-focused health system affiliated with the University of Minnesota and providing a complete range of services, from the prevention of illness and injury to care for the most complex medical conditions. For a free current catalog of Fairview Press titles, call toll-free 1-800-544-8207. Or visit www.fairviewpress.org.

Library of Congress Cataloging-in-Publication Data
The new family : your child's first year / by Fairview Health Services.
    p. cm.
  ISBN 1-57749-146-7 (trade pbk. : alk. paper)
  1. Infants--Development. 2. Infants--Care. 3. Parent and infant. I.
Fairview Health Services.
  RJ134.N493 2004
  649'.122--dc22
                                    2003016467

First printing: January 2004
Printed in the United States of America
08 07 06 05 04   6 5 4 3 2 1

Writer: Linda Picone
General editor: Lora Harding-Dundek
Book designer: Jane Dahms Nicolo
Illustrator: Barbara Beshoar

Acknowledgments
Many individuals from Fairview Health Services contributed to this project. They include Dalia Abrams, BSc, MA, CCE; Jody Arman-Jones, BsEd, CCE; Nancy Barkley, RN; Judy Cannon, RNC, MS; Deb Cathcart, RN, MS; Linda DiBartolo, RNC; Kathy Eide, RN, NP; Mary Ess, RN, IBCLC; Donna J. Florence, MS, RN, ACCE, CNS; Patricia Fontaine, MD; Laurie Frattallone, BA; Becky Gams, RNC; Kay Gray, BA, BS; Judy Grumm, RN; Margaret Harder, CCRN, BSN, MA; Lora Harding-Dundek, BA, MPH, ICCE; Jeanne Hartwig, LPN; Debra Heaver, RN; Jane Helgesen, RN, IBCLC; Debra Johnson, RN; Kathryn Kerber, RN, MS, CNS; Evelyn Lindholm, RN, IBCLC; Kathleen Maloney, RN; Rachel McCann, RN; Laurie McNamara, RN; Bonnie Miller, RN; Patti Mortland, RN, CNNP; Kim Mullon, RN; Sue Nesheim, RN; Denise Palmer, RN, MS; Lorina Patterson, parent advisor; Vicki Pieper, RN, IBCLC; Jeri Price, BA, CCE; Wendy Raisir, parent advisor; Jane Rauenhorst, MALP; Marie Root, RN, IBCLE; Ann Shelp, BSN, ICCE; Anthony Shibley, MD; Arlyce Shook, RNC; Noreen Siebenaler, RN, MSN, IBCLC; Patti Sollinger, MSN, CPNP; Sheryl Lynds Stowman, MDiv, ACPE Supervisor; and Aner Vladaver, MD. We thank our patients and their families and the many other people who helped move this book from conception to reality.

Contents

Introduction

This book—together with its companion volume, *The Expectant Family: From Pregnancy through Childbirth*—is designed to provide the basic information you need to make the best decisions possible about pregnancy, labor, birth, and parenting. For additional information, you will find recommended resources listed at the end of most chapters.

You may, at times, feel overwhelmed with all the information and resources available to help you prepare for and parent your baby. You may wonder, "What is it that I need to know?"

To answer this general question, try to imagine yourself in specific situations:

- Once your baby is born, do you imagine yourself and your baby together throughout your hospital stay, or is the baby in the nursery? How do you picture yourself feeding your baby?

- When you come home from the hospital with your baby, who do you picture being with you? Will you want extra help at home, or time alone as a family?

- How do you picture the first weeks at home with your baby? Is the baby sleeping a lot? How often is the baby eating? What information do you need to make these images clearer?

Thinking about specific situations such as these will lead you to ask the questions that you really need answered. Together, both *The Expectant Family* and *The New Family* will bring clarity to your thoughts and help you find the answers to your questions.

In addition to the advice offered in these books, you will also receive information and guidance from health care providers. Health care providers may include physicians, certified nurse-midwives, nurses, or nurse practitioners. You may also spend time with a childbirth educator or doula. The relationships you form with the people providing direct care to you and your baby are very important. Together, these health care providers will give you the resources you need to have a healthy pregnancy and a healthy baby.

1 *Your Newborn*

This tiny creature in your arms is your baby—an independent little person who is already capable of many things. You are excited and scared. Who is this little person?

New parents often think they need to know everything about caring for their baby before they leave the hospital. The exhaustion that comes with becoming a parent makes this impossible. However, you can learn a great deal simply by observing your newborn.

SOME OF THE QUESTIONS ANSWERED
IN THIS CHAPTER INCLUDE:

- What can my baby see and hear?
- How do I give my baby a bath?
- What does my baby's crying mean?
- How do I make sure the baby's crib is safe?
- When do I call my baby's health care provider?

A First Look at Your Newborn

YOU MAY THINK your newborn is the most beautiful baby—the most beautiful anything—you've ever seen. Then again, you might not. This baby may look very different from the baby you had imagined when you were pregnant. His or her head may have been squeezed into a long shape during the birth process. Or, if forceps were used, there may be red marks on the sides of your baby's head. Maybe your baby has long, fine hair over his or her body.

These characteristics are all completely normal—and temporary. The forceps marks will fade away and the baby's head will round into a normal shape in a few days. The long, fine hair, called **lanugo**, will disappear in about a week.

Other things you may notice about your newborn:

Head

- There are soft spots on the top and at the back of your baby's head, where the bones still haven't grown together. These soft spots may make you a little nervous about touching your baby's head. You need to be gentle, but you can still wash your baby's hair or massage your baby's head and scalp.
- There may be a soft, spongy area on your baby's head, caused by the pressure of birth. This will go away in a few days. Some babies have a hard knot on the top of their head, called a **cephalhematoma**. This will also go away, although it may take 4 to 6 months.

Eyes

- Light-skinned babies usually have grayish-blue eyes when they are born. Dark-skinned babies usually have grayish-brown eyes. Your baby's true eye color may appear in a few months, or may take as long as a year to develop. The color of your baby's eyes doesn't have anything to do with the ability to see.

NOSE

- Some babies are born with a nose that looks squished. The nose will develop normally in a short time.
- Your baby may sneeze a lot. The inside of the nose is much smaller than the nostrils you see, so mucus catches easily. Sneezing clears the nasal passages so the baby can breathe.

SKIN

- Small white bumps called **milia** are common on the face. Just leave them alone—don't try to squeeze or pick at them—and they will disappear in a few weeks.
- Some babies will have a newborn rash on their bodies. It will disappear in about a week.
- Dark-skinned babies may have a darker area on their buttocks, back, or genitals that can be present for 4 or 5 years. This **Mongolian Spot** is not harmful and doesn't hurt, even though it may look like a bruise.
- **Jaundice,** or yellowish skin, is common in newborns. Call your care provider if your baby's skin is very yellow or if the whites of his or her eyes are yellow.

GENITALS

- Both boy and girl babies usually have swollen genitals. This is sometimes startling to parents, but it's normal and the swelling goes down in a few days.

Some of the unusual marks you notice on your newborn baby's body, such as a squished nose or Mongolian Spots, are normal and will change or disappear as your baby matures.

WHAT YOUR NEWBORN CAN DO

YOUR BABY was born with the ability to do a number of things. You'll enjoy watching and playing with your baby, and your attention will help your baby develop.

WHAT YOUR BABY CAN SEE

- When first born, a baby can see about a foot away. (Be sure to dim the lights—bright lights make it more difficult for your newborn to see.) By the time the baby is 4 to 6 months old, he or she can see as well as an adult. Babies like faces, so looking into your baby's eyes and talking will often fascinate your baby.
- Babies can get overwhelmed by having too much to look at. Keep your baby's sleeping area uncluttered. Very bright colors in decorating or bedding can be too exciting for a new baby.

What can my baby see and hear?

WHAT YOUR BABY CAN HEAR

- When you were about 24 weeks pregnant, your baby started to hear your voice inside the uterus. When your baby is born, he or she can hear as well as an adult.
- Your baby will get used to the normal sounds of your household; no one needs to tiptoe or whisper.
- The high-pitched "baby talk" voice we often use with babies is something they seem to like. A baby will turn toward someone using that voice and study the speaker's face.

WHAT YOUR BABY CAN SMELL AND TASTE

- Newborn babies can smell as well as adults, and their sense of taste is even stronger than that of adults.
- A baby will turn away from sharp, unpleasant odors.
- Babies like sweet things; however, you should never add sugar to a baby's formula or water, because it can cause diarrhea.

WHAT YOUR BABY CAN FEEL

- Babies need to be held, to feel close to someone, and to be touched by loving hands. Fussiness with diaper changes or baths is normal; don't let it keep you from holding your baby.
- Babies cannot be "spoiled," so hold and carry your baby often. The warmth of your body, and your particular scent, are very soothing.

WHAT YOUR BABY'S BEHAVIORS MEAN

- Babies often suck on their fingers or fist to comfort themselves. If you place your finger in the palm of your baby's hand, the baby's fingers will curl around your finger. This is the **grasp reflex.** You can then bring your baby's fist to his or her mouth.

- When you change your baby's diaper or clean the umbilical cord, your baby may start to cry. You are not hurting your baby; your baby is simply cold. Crying increases body temperature. You may want to keep your baby partially covered when you change a diaper, clean the umbilical cord, or give the baby a bath.

- When you pick your baby up, the baby may open his or her mouth or turn his or her head from side to side. This is a natural reflex to help your baby search for the nipple. If you stroke your baby's cheek, the baby's head will turn toward the side you touched. Your baby may begin to suck, or he or she may wait until a nipple is offered. This is called the **sucking and rooting reflex,** which helps your baby attach to the nipple.

- When your baby looks or turns away while being held, flushes red, or grows pale around the lips, the baby may be ready to stop whatever he or she is doing. Your baby may start to yawn, frown, or sneeze to let you know that he or she is ready to do something else. Your baby may do these things before crying to let you know that he or she needs your help.

- When awake, your baby may turn and look right at you. The baby's body will be still; his or her eyes will be wide and clear. These are signs that your baby is ready to engage with you. Your newborn will study your face, watch you speak, and appear to understand everything you say. During the first few weeks, this might occur only a few minutes each day.

CIRCUMCISION

YOU MAY WISH to have your baby boy's penis circumcised. In this procedure, the foreskin—the skin that covers the head of the penis—is cut away. Some parents choose circumcision for religious reasons, others because they think it is the "usual" thing to do.

Although physicians once routinely recommended circumcision for health reasons, many physicians now see it as an elective procedure—one that parents may choose, but that is not necessary for the baby's health. If you are considering circumcision, ask your health care provider to talk with you about the risks and the current medical thinking.

If you choose to have your baby circumcised, the procedure usually will be done before you leave the hospital. The surgery takes about 10 minutes, and healing generally takes about a week.

KEEPING YOUR BABY CLEAN

YOUR NEWBORN only needs to be bathed once or twice a week, but you need to clean his or her bottom throughout the day and comb the scalp once a day.

CORD CARE

- Once each day, look at the area where the cord is attached. If the cord looks red, you notice a bad smell, or you see pus in the cord area, call your health care provider. These are signs of an infection.

- The cord will fall off in about 1–3 weeks. If you want, you can clean the cord area once a day. The cord may fall off sooner if you do this. To clean the cord and the cord area, first wash your hands, then dip a cotton swab in alcohol, or use an alcohol wipe. Very gently rub around the base of the cord. Pull the cord up and push the cotton swab gently into the base to remove any secretions.

- To keep the cord dry, fold the diaper below the cord during the first few weeks.

NAIL CARE

- Babies' fingernails can be sharp. They are very soft and hard to cut for at least 2 to 3 weeks. You can gently file them.

GENITAL CARE

- Girls sometimes have a small pink or white discharge from the vagina. This is normal and nothing to worry about. Always wash a girl's genital area from front to back.

- If your baby boy is circumcised, follow the instructions given to you by your baby's health care provider. If you notice bleeding or pus, or if your baby seems to be having trouble passing urine, contact your health care provider immediately.

- If your baby is not circumcised, clean the penis gently with water, but do not pull on the foreskin.

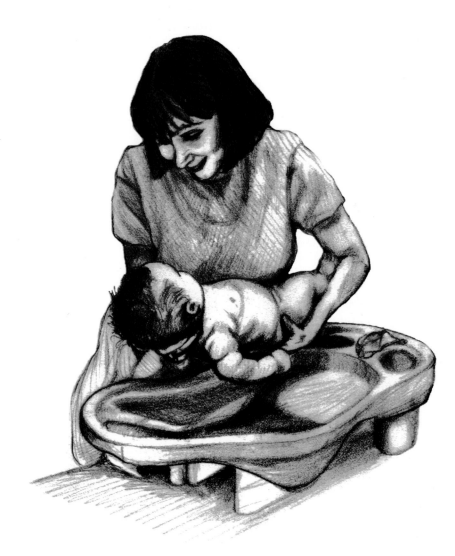

Support your baby's head as you lower the baby into a basin or tub and as you gently bathe each part of your baby's body.

GIVING YOUR BABY A BATH

Whether your baby is being bathed in water or while lying on a safe surface, you should make sure he or she doesn't get chilled. Keep the area warm, and wrap your baby in warm, dry clothes right after the bath.

1. Gather bath supplies together. These include:
   - mild soap (although you can bathe your baby in warm water without soap)
   - alcohol and cotton swabs
   - comb and brush
   - clean diaper
   - clean clothes
   - washcloth and towels
   - pan or sink for water
   - a safe surface, with a blanket or pad

2. Test the water for the bath. It should be warm, but not hot. Use your elbow to check for a safe water temperature. Never put your baby into a bath without checking the water first.

3. While supporting your baby's head with your hand, lower your baby's body into the water.

4. Wash around the eyes first with plain water. Then wash the face with plain water. Don't use cotton swabs to clean your baby's nose or ears.

5. Wash the baby's hair with plain water or with water and a mild shampoo. After the bath, comb your baby's scalp to remove oily build-up.

6. Wash your baby's stomach, back, and hands with plain water. Clean between your baby's fingers, and pay special attention to creases in the skin, such as around the neck area or armpits.

7. Wash the legs and feet, including between the toes.

8. Wash the baby's bottom from front to back with water and mild soap.

How do I give my baby a bath?

TAKING YOUR BABY'S TEMPERATURE

ALTHOUGH A **rectal temperature** is more accurate, it is safer and easier to take an **axillary (underarm) temperature** for a newborn.

The axillary temperature is taken by tucking the thermometer into your baby's bare armpit and holding the arm gently against the chest. Hold the thermometer this way for at least 4 minutes. An average axillary temperature is 97.6° F.

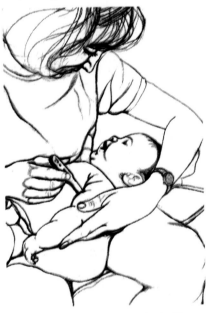

Take an axillary temperature by tucking the thermometer into your baby's bare armpit.

For a rectal temperature, lubricate the tip of a rectal thermometer (specially made, with a small, round bulb at the end) with petroleum jelly. Put your baby on his or her stomach, with a diaper underneath. (Taking a rectal temperature is likely to cause a bowel movement.) Or put the baby on his or her back and lift the baby's legs with one hand while pushing apart the buttocks with the other enough to see the rectum. Insert the thermometer gently, about a half inch. Hold it in place for about 3 minutes. An average rectal temperature is 99.6° F.

Take a rectal temperature by putting just the tip of a rectal thermometer into the baby's rectum.

YOUR BABY'S STATES OF CONSCIOUSNESS

YOUR BABY has six states of consciousness. Understanding them will help you better respond to and care for you baby.

- **Deep sleep.** Breathing is steady and regular. You do not see any eye movement. Noise does not disturb your baby, although it may cause the baby to move in his or her sleep. Your baby is not available to you in this state.
- **Light sleep.** Breathing seems faster, and your baby's chest rises and falls with each breath. You notice movement beneath his or her closed eyelids. The baby may move around and even suck in his or her sleep. Your baby is more available for feeding because he or she is closer to being awake.
- **Drowsy or semi-dozing.** Your baby's eyes are open, but he or she stares into space, not focusing on anything in particular. Your baby may decide to wake up or go back to sleep.
- **Quiet alert.** Your baby's eyes are wide open, bright, and alert. The baby will not move his or her body much and will stay focused on whatever he or she is looking at. Your baby is most available to you in this state.
- **Active alert.** Your baby is fussy. He or she moves around and may cry out briefly. In this state, your baby is more sensitive to hunger, sleepiness, or being handled.
- **Crying.** When your baby cries, the baby is telling you that he or she needs something. The baby may be ready to eat, have a diaper changed, be burped, or be held and comforted.

Newborns have the ability to shut out repeated noise and stimuli when they are in a deep sleep, light sleep, or drowsy state. This is called **habituation.** This allows families to carry on with their daily activities without disturbing their baby.

The first few hours after your baby is born, he or she will most likely be in a quiet-alert state. Your baby will want to spend time watching your face and listening to your voice.

For the next 24 to 36 hours, your baby will spend a lot of time sleeping. As feeding time approaches, look for signs that your baby is in a light sleep. If your baby is in a deep sleep, it will be difficult to get him or her to suck on the breast or bottle.

When your baby is 3 to 4 days old, he or she will start to cycle between deep and light sleep every 30 to 40 minutes. It will be easier to anticipate when your baby is available for feeding.

BABY'S CRYING

NEWBORN BABIES tell you what they want by crying. They cry when they're hungry, tired, or uncomfortable. They cry when they've had too much excitement or not enough.

You can expect your baby to cry about 2 or 3 hours out of every day. Some days it may be more, and some days it may be less. Some things to remember:

- **Your baby cries because that's how he or she communicates.**
- **Responding to your baby's cries now may mean less crying in the future.**
- **A newborn baby can't be "spoiled" if you pick him or her up.** In some cultures, babies are held almost constantly by their mothers. Studies show that babies who are kept closer to Mom or Dad actually cry less.
- **Your baby is different than anyone else's baby.** While some ways of dealing with crying may have worked for your sister's baby or your next-door neighbor's baby, you have to learn what your baby needs.
- **Never handle your baby when you're feeling angry or frustrated.** Put the baby in a safe place, or let someone else hold the baby for a while, and then walk away and calm down.
- **Never shake your baby.**

What does my baby's crying mean?

THINGS YOU CAN TRY TO EASE YOUR BABY'S CRYING

- **Feed your baby.** Yes, even if it's only been a short time since the last feeding. Your baby has his or her own schedule that doesn't always follow a clock. Frequent feeding is normal.
- **Rub the baby's tummy, or lay the baby over your arm or lap and rub his or her back.**
- **Get out the rocking chair.** Rock the baby, or walk around the room while holding the baby.
- **Check the baby's clothing.** Add a layer if it's chilly; take a layer off if it's hot. Also, check to see if the baby's diaper needs to be changed.
- **Take a ride in the car, with the baby safely buckled into the infant car seat in the back.**
- **Understand that sometimes your baby may cry to "blow off steam."** This is normal. When this happens, stay with your baby. He or she needs to know you are there. You might put the baby down on the floor or couch while you sit next to him or her and observe how the baby tries to comfort himself or herself. For instance, if you see the baby trying to suck on his or her fist or fingers, you can assist the baby by using the grasp reflex. (See page 7.)
- **If you feel overwhelmed, call a friend or neighbor to watch the baby until you feel better.**

NEWBORN SAFETY

YOU CAN HELP keep your baby safe by following these guidelines:

- **Always use a federally-approved car seat**—even when you give your baby his or her first ride home from the hospital. The safest place for the car seat is in the middle of the backseat, facing the rear of the car. Yes, that can be awkward, but it is one of the most important things you can do for your baby. *Never* hold your baby on your lap in a moving car.

- **Never leave your baby alone in a vehicle.** Not even "just for a minute" as you run into the house or a store to pick something up.

- **Never leave your baby alone on a high, flat surface, like the top of a dresser or changing table.** Even a very tiny baby can scoot across a flat surface if its feet find something to push against.

- **Put your baby to sleep on his or her back, not on the tummy.** Recent research has shown that babies who sleep on their sides or backs are less likely to have Sudden Infant Death Syndrome (SIDS).

- **Make sure your baby's crib is safe.** It should have slats that are no more than 2 3/8 inches apart, and the mattress should fit snugly against the edge of the crib—you should not be able to fit 2 fingers between the mattress and the side of the crib. If the crib is painted, make sure that lead-free paint was used. If you don't know, it's better to get a newer crib. Don't use bumper pads or pillows in the crib; babies can be suffocated in their soft surfaces. No toys should be left in the crib with a newborn. Keep the crib away from windows, plants, drapes, electric cords, or anything that the baby might be able to grasp.

- **Only use store-bought pacifiers.** This is one item that you should not try to make at home. Check the pacifier often by pulling on the bulb to make sure it's not loose, sticky, or cracked. If it is, replace it immediately.

How do I make sure the baby's crib is safe?

- **Never prop a bottle for the baby to eat.** Always hold your baby while feeding.
- **Never microwave formula or breast milk.** It heats unevenly and may burn the inside of your baby's mouth.
- **Keep your baby out of direct sunlight—a newborn's skin is very sensitive—and don't use insect repellent or sunscreen on your baby for at least six months.**
- **Don't drink hot beverages, eat hot food, or smoke while holding your baby.**
- **Don't smoke around your baby.** Secondhand smoke can cause illnesses, including ear infections and breathing problems.

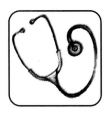

When do I call my
health care provider?

CLINIC VISITS

IF YOU HAVEN'T picked a health care provider for your baby
before birth, you should pick one as soon as your baby is born.

A visit to the health care provider usually is scheduled for 2
weeks after the baby is born. At this visit, the health care
provider will give you a schedule for regular checkups for your
baby, including the immunizations he or she will need.

WHEN TO CALL YOUR HEALTH CARE PROVIDER

You may not be sure when your baby is sick and needs to see
a health care provider, especially if this is your first baby. Some
signs that your baby should see someone are:

- **An underarm (axillary) temperature higher than 100.5° F,
  or a rectal temperature higher than 101° F.**
- **Changes in your baby's behavior.** For example, a normally
  quiet baby is very fussy and irritable all day, or an active
  baby is very sleepy and limp.
- **Vomiting.** This is not spitting up after feedings, which is
  normal, but actually vomiting stomach contents.
- **Diarrhea or constipation.**
- **If your baby's skin seems yellow and your baby is very sleepy.**
- **If your baby's skin seems bluish, or if your baby starts
  coughing.**
- **If your baby is uninterested in feeding for more than 6 to 8
  hours or has less than 6 wet diapers in a 24-hour period.**

Don't hesitate to call your health care provider if you are
concerned about your baby's health. No one will think you're
foolish if you ask for help.

Neonatal Intensive Care Unit (NICU)

IF YOUR BABY needs special care, he or she will be taken care of in the intensive care nursery or special care unit, where the extra care gives your baby a better chance at a healthy future.

When you first look at the neonatal intensive care unit (NICU), you may think the machines and lights and sounds are frightening. The high-tech equipment doesn't look like what you thought would be your baby's first environment, but it's all there to meet your baby's special needs and to monitor his or her condition.

While your baby is in the NICU, the staff will provide you with information so you will understand what is happening to your baby and how well your baby is doing.

FOR PARTNERS

EXCEPT FOR breastfeeding, you can do everything your partner does now. You can hold, bathe, and diaper the baby. You can talk to him or her, hold the baby in your arms, or carry the baby in a front pack against your chest. You can make sure the baby is buckled into a babyseat when you're in the car, and you can check the baby's crib to make sure it's safe. And, if the baby is taking formula, you can even help feed the baby.

Get to know the baby, and the basics of baby care, so you can be actively involved in taking care of the baby. This will give your partner some relief, and it will be good for the baby. But you'll also find that it is good for you, too.

FOR MORE INFORMATION

Your Amazing Newborn by Marshall H. Klaus, MD, and
  Phyllis Klaus.
The Baby Book by William Sears, MD, and Martha Sears.
Caring for Your Baby and Young Child by American Academy of
  Pediatrics.
Consumer Reports Guide to Baby Products by Sandy Jones.
On Becoming A Family by T. Berry Brazelton.
Touchpoints by T. Berry Brazelton.
What Every Baby Knows by T. Berry Brazelton.
You and Your Newborn Baby by Linda Todd.

Consumer Reports <www.consumerreports.org>.

Feeding Your Baby

Your breast milk is the best source of nutrition for your baby. Nursing can make you feel closer to your baby, and it will make your baby feel protected and safe.

Although most women breastfeed their babies, some choose not to, and a very few cannot, for physical and other reasons. With prepared formula, you can still provide your baby with a loving, warm experience while feeding.

SOME OF THE QUESTIONS ANSWERED
IN THIS CHAPTER INCLUDE:

- What are the advantages of breastfeeding?
- How often should I nurse my baby?
- What should I do if I cannot be with my baby at feeding time?
- What problems might arise during breastfeeding?
- What should I know about formula feeding?

BREASTFEEDING

BREASTFEEDING IS the natural, healthy way to feed your baby. Studies show that breastfed babies are less likely to get colds, ear infections, and other illnesses. Breastfeeding lowers a baby's risk of Sudden Infant Death Syndrome (SIDS) and other health problems including diabetes, allergies, asthma, and weight gain in later life. Breast milk contains fatty acids that may promote healthy brain development. The American Academy of Pediatrics recommends that all babies be breastfed for at least the first year.

Mothers benefit from breastfeeding as well. Women's bodies are designed for breastfeeding, and most women find it to be a satisfying experience. Breastfeeding helps control bleeding after childbirth, and it lowers the risk of premenopausal breast cancer, ovarian cancer, and osteoporosis. It also stimulates hormones in a woman's body that promote feelings of relaxation and well-being. Finally, using breast milk instead of formula can save $1500 a year!

Breastfeeding for just a few weeks—or alternating breast milk and formula—is healthier than not breastfeeding at all. Many women continue to breastfeed after they return to work. Breast pumps make it easy to save milk for your baby, whether you can be there for every feeding or not. Several states have laws protecting a woman's right to pump breast milk at work for later feedings.

Although breastfeeding is natural, it is a skill that you and your baby must learn. After all, neither of you has done it before! Before your baby is born, attend a breastfeeding class sponsored by your local hospital or La Leche League. Be sure to bring a partner or other support person to class. You'll both benefit from the information and encouragement.

After your baby is born, you can practice breastfeeding skills by staying together as much as possible, especially at night. Babies often do their best feeding at night, so take advantage of late-night feeding opportunities. Some studies show that mothers and babies actually sleep better when they sleep together, and this will make nighttime feedings easier. If the hospital nurses bottlefeed your baby, your breasts will not be stimulated throughout the night, which increases your chances of engorgement and low milk supply.

THE BREAST

Your breasts changed a lot while you were pregnant. They became larger and more tender. These changes were caused by the growth of milk-producing cells and an increase in blood flow to the breasts. If you have light skin, you may be able to see blue veins in your breasts now. Your nipples may have gotten much bigger and darker, and some bumps may have appeared in the darker area around the nipple. These bumps are actually small glands that help keep your nipples soft and protected from bacteria when you are nursing. Soap can destroy this protective effect, so wash your breasts only with warm water when you bathe.

Some women have a slight leakage of milk from their breasts in the last months of pregnancy. This thick yellowish milk, **colostrum,** is the first food your baby will have. Your breasts are producing it, even if you don't see it before your baby is born.

After your baby is born, your breasts will produce colostrum for several days. Colostrum gives your newborn many advantages, including protection against many diseases. It also helps your baby pass **meconium,** the first black, tarry bowel movements.

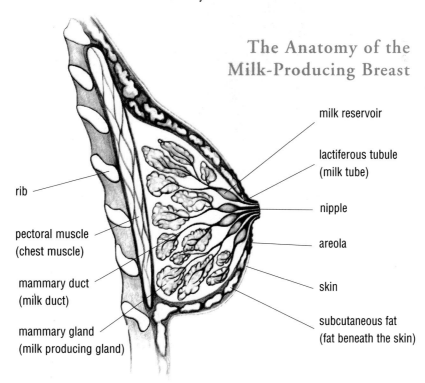

The Anatomy of the
Milk-Producing Breast

milk reservoir

lactiferous tubule
(milk tube)

rib

nipple

pectoral muscle
(chest muscle)

areola

mammary duct
(milk duct)

skin

mammary gland
(milk producing gland)

subcutaneous fat
(fat beneath the skin)

Milk is produced in special cells of the breast, then released through the nipple. A special hormone called oxytocin causes the milk to be released. This effect is called the **let-down reflex.** Two to four days after the baby is born, your breasts will start to feel fuller and heavier as your milk production increases. Frequent feedings will prevent your breasts from overfilling (commonly known as engorgement).

GETTING STARTED

MOST BABIES are able to nurse at birth, but they sometimes need a little help getting started. Your baby may not be interested right away. That's okay. You can begin simply by holding the baby near your breast and letting the baby lick or touch your nipple. Skin-to-skin cuddling is a great way to spend time with your baby. It's also a wonderful activity for your partner and the baby. It will help your baby get ready to breastfeed.

To help get started with breastfeeding, there are several steps that may be helpful:

- **Get comfortable.** A padded chair may be more comfortable than the hospital bed. Keep plenty of pillows handy.
- **Hold your baby so that his or her tummy faces your tummy.** Use pillows to support your arms in a comfortable position. Sit up straight. Bring the baby to your breast instead of bringing your breast to the baby.
- **Present your breast to the baby.** Hold your breast, usually with your thumb on top and your fingers underneath, so your hand forms a "C" shape well behind the areola. The palm of your hand will rest under your breast.
- **Pull your baby in close to your body.** Remember to maintain the tummy-to-tummy position.
- **Get your baby to open his or her mouth.** Gently rub your nipple across the baby's lower lip. If you open your mouth wide and say "ah," your baby will learn to mimic you.
- **Quickly move the baby deeply onto the breast.** Repeat this step until the baby latches on and begins to suck. Don't lean

To begin breastfeeding, find a comfortable position for you and your baby, with your back and arms supported. Bending your leg into a chair or using a footstool can help.

toward the baby. Be sure your baby's nose, chest, and knees are touching you.

- **The baby's mouth should be wide open on the breast.** You should feel a strong pull when the baby sucks. You should not feel pain. Have your nurse or partner carefully check if the baby's lower lip is turned outward. The lower lip should be on the areola, at least half an inch from the base of the nipple.

Use your free hand to partially circle the breast and guide it into your baby's mouth. Make sure you bring your baby deeply onto the breast.

- **Take the baby off the breast if the baby hasn't latched on properly.** Signs that the baby has not latched on correctly include: little or no suction, smacking or clicking sounds, lips that are close together, dimples in the baby's cheeks with every suck, visibility of most of the areola, and nipple pain that does not decrease as the baby nurses.
- **Listen for swallowing.** After a few minutes, you may start to hear swallowing. This is a sign of milk release, or let-down. To encourage milk release, relax, imagine your milk flowing to your baby, or sing or talk to your baby.
- **Break suction carefully to take your baby off the breast.** Never pull your baby away from your breast without breaking the suction. Put your finger into the corner of the baby's mouth between his or her gums and gently break the suction.

BREASTFEEDING POSITIONS

There are a number of positions for breastfeeding. Try several and see which are most comfortable for you and your baby. Some babies and mothers will come to prefer one position to the others.

Cradle Hold

This is the classic position for breastfeeding. In this position, you cradle your baby's head in the crook of the arm on the same side as the breast. If your baby is nursing from the left breast, his or her head will be resting in the crook of your left arm. Use your other hand to lift your breast, partly circling the nipple with the thumb on top and fingers underneath. Touch your baby's lip or the side of the mouth with the nipple so that he or she will open the mouth toward the breast. Bring your baby's head in toward your breast by moving the bent arm in (don't lean into the baby; it may make your back ache).

In this position, you hold the baby's neck and the back of your baby's head in the hand that is opposite to the breast being used, while the baby's body lies across your body. If your baby is nursing at the left breast, your right hand will be holding the baby's head and the baby's feet will be on your right side. Put the baby's face in front of your breast and use your free hand to hold your breast. Put your thumb slightly to the side, a little more than an inch from your nipple, and your index finger opposite the thumb. Touch your baby's lip or the side of the mouth with the nipple so that he or she will open the mouth toward the breast. Then move the baby's head in toward you until he or she begins to suck.

Cross Cradle Hold

Football Hold

The football hold keeps the baby's weight off your abdomen, so it can be especially good after a cesarean birth. With your baby facing you, hold his or her whole body, including the back of the neck and head, with the hand on the same side as the breast being used. If your baby is nursing from the left breast, your left hand should hold the baby, while the baby's bottom goes against the bed or chair you are sitting on, and the baby's feet are toward the back of the bed or chair. Use the opposite hand to lift the breast, with the thumb on top of the nipple and the index finger below. Touch your baby's lip with the nipple so that he or she will open the mouth toward the breast. Then move the baby's head in toward you until he or she begins to suck.

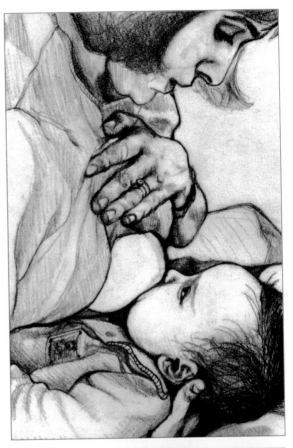

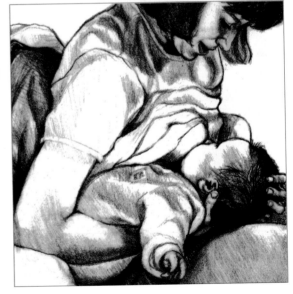

Side-Lying Position

Lying on your side, place your baby on the side also, so that the baby's face is toward your breast. If you are on your left side, your baby will be on his or her right side. Bring your left arm straight down under the baby, holding him or her close to you. You might need to put a pillow under your baby to make this more comfortable for both of you. Use your opposite hand to lift the breast, with the thumb on top of the nipple and the index finger below. Touch your baby's lip with the nipple so that he or she will open the mouth toward the breast. Then move the baby's head in toward you until he or she begins to suck.

Breastfeeding Twins

If you have twins, you may sometimes nurse both of them at the same time. You can do this most easily with the football hold, the cradle hold, or a combination of the two. The hardest part of nursing two babies at once is getting each one started nursing on a breast. You may need help in the early weeks.

How Often to Nurse Your Baby

Especially at first, your baby needs to be in charge of how often you nurse and for how long. As your baby grows and your milk supply increases, the baby will take in more milk at each feeding, and the feedings will become further apart.

Newborns usually nurse 8 to 12 times in 24 hours, or approximately every 1½ to 3 hours each day. Like adults, babies need to be fed when they are hungry, and they are not necessarily hungry at predictable times. Some babies will group several feedings close together and then wait awhile before feeding again. This is called "cluster feeding."

It is important to watch your baby for signs of hunger. If your baby sucks on his or her fingers, makes mouth movements, or turns toward the breast when held, your baby is asking to be fed. If the baby is not fed, he or she will begin to cry. Crying is a late sign of hunger.

Some babies do not ask to be fed often enough. If your baby is not eating at least 8 times in a 24-hour period, you may need to initiate more feedings, even when your baby shows no signs of hunger.

At first, your baby may fall asleep during breastfeeding, doze for a while, and then wake up to suck some more. You can help your baby wake up by stimulating his or her feet, back, or legs. Always allow your baby to finish the first breast. When the baby releases the nipple or has gotten sleepy, burp the baby and then offer the second breast. Some babies fill up on just one side. This is perfectly normal. At the next feeding, start with the other breast.

Newborn babies tend to nurse more often than their parents expect. Frequent, long feedings (10 to 30 minutes) in the early days will increase your milk supply faster, stimulate your baby's immune system, help the baby gain weight sooner, limit the risk of jaundice, and lower the risk of engorgement. Years ago, mothers were advised to nurse no more than a few minutes on each breast in order to prevent sore, cracked nipples. Now we know that sore nipples are not caused by long feeding sessions, but by a baby incorrectly latching onto the nipple.

How often should I nurse my baby?

By 6 weeks of age, many babies nurse every 2 to 3 hours, sometimes "clustering" feedings in the evening and sleeping more during the night. If your 6-week-old baby feeds more at night, you may want to try waking the baby several times during the day to eat. After awhile, his or her feeding schedule will change. For the next several months, your baby may continue to wake up at least once during the night for feeding. This is perfectly normal.

Besides the strong sucking they use to get their milk, some babies also engage in gentle sucking to satisfy a basic need for closeness and comfort. If you and your baby enjoy this closeness, it is okay to let the sucking continue. However, if your nipples are sore, you may want to limit "comfort sucking" until they heal. (See page 15 for ideas on comforting your baby.)

Nursing at Home

- **Have a calm, pleasant place to breastfeed.** Set up a nursing area in a relatively quiet part of the house, and use a chair that is comfortable for you with a baby in your arms. The chair or sofa should be padded enough so you can get into a comfortable position and sit for a while.
- **When you sit down to nurse, have a glass of milk, juice, or water within reach.** You may be more thirsty when you are nursing.
- **Keep a phone close by so you don't have to jump up when it rings.**

Nursing in Public

It may be hard to imagine nursing your baby in public. If you are uncomfortable with the thought of breastfeeding your baby outside your home, that's okay. Some women choose to pump their breast milk and store it in bottles for public feedings.

Some women, however, become quite comfortable breastfeeding their babies anywhere. Practice—and perhaps the use of oversized shirts and baby blankets—make public breastfeeding a natural, healthy, and convenient option for many women.

Burping Your Baby

Your baby may swallow some air while nursing or crying. This can make the baby uncomfortable, so you may want to burp the baby whenever you change breasts during a feeding, and then perhaps again after a feeding.

Don't worry if your baby doesn't burp. Breastfed babies tend to swallow less air than bottlefed babies, so they may need to burp less often, especially during the first few days.

The most common burping position is holding the baby high on your shoulder as you pat his or her back. You may find this is the most natural and comfortable position for you, but there are others you can try as well:

- Sit the baby on your lap, facing sideways. Support the baby's head with one hand just under the jaw while you gently pat or rub your baby on the lower back.
- Rest the baby on his or her stomach, across your knees, and pat or rub the baby's back.

Your baby may burp up some milk along with the air. This is nothing to worry about. However, your baby may vomit what seems like a whole feeding, rather than just spitting up a little milk. If this happens more than once, or if the milk shoots out forcefully, you should call your health care provider, especially if your baby also has a fever.

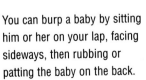

You can burp a baby by sitting him or her on your lap, facing sideways, then rubbing or patting the baby on the back.

How to Tell if Your Baby Is Getting Enough Milk

If your baby is about one week old, use the following checklist to be sure that he or she is getting enough milk:

___ You are breastfeeding the baby at least 8 to 12 times in 24 hours.

___ You can hear the baby swallow while breastfeeding.

___ Your breasts are fuller before a feeding and softer afterward.

___ The baby is producing at least six wet diapers in 24 hours.

___ The baby is producing four or more yellow bowel movements the size of a quarter or larger in 24 hours.

___ The baby is content for a while between some of the feedings.

___ The baby is gaining weight. (If in doubt, call your baby's health care provider for a weight check.)

___ The baby is alert and responsive during awake periods.

Breastfeeding works on a supply-and-demand basis. If you nurse whenever the baby asks to be fed, usually from 8 to 12 times in a 24-hour period, then you almost certainly will make plenty of milk. If you try to feed on a rigid schedule or limit the time the baby is at the breast, your milk supply may decrease. To make more milk, feed frequently and allow the baby as much time as he or she wants on the breast.

As your baby grows, he or she will drink more milk. There will be days when you feel like all you do is breastfeed. Growth spurts occur around 2 to 3 weeks, 6 weeks, 3 months, and 6 months. During these times, your baby may not seem satisfied. You may feel like you have lost your milk or that your milk is inadequate. Nearly all nursing mothers experience this. Simply nurse longer and more often, and after a day or two, your milk supply will increase. Good nutrition, along with as much rest as you can manage, will help keep you and your milk supply healthy.

Use the breastfeeding log on the following pages. If you think that your baby isn't getting enough milk during the first week, call your care provider, lactation consultant, or La Leche League.

Breastfeeding When Your Baby Is in the NICU

Your baby may come to the NICU (Neonatal Intensive Care Unit) for many different reasons. Your baby may be born early (premature), be sick with an infection, need surgery, or struggle with breathing problems. Whatever the reason, you may wonder if you will be able to breastfeed your baby. While your baby's health will be a factor, you will most likely be able to breastfeed. How and when you are able to bring your baby to the breast will depend on why your baby is in the NICU.

Even though you may not be able to bring your baby to the breast right away, your body is still ready to feed your baby. Instead of your baby coming to the breast 8 to 10 times in 24 hours, you will use a high-quality electric breast pump to pump the colostrum and then the breast milk from your breasts. The pumping will allow you to build a full milk supply so that when your baby is ready to breastfeed the breastmilk will be available.

As your baby gets better, he or she will begin to come to the breast for feedings. These feedings may be short and infrequent. You will continue to pump your breasts as your baby gains strength and increases the length and frequency of feedings at the breast.

While your baby is in the NICU, a lactation consultant will help you with pumping and any additional assistance that your baby may need with breastfeeding. When your baby is ready to leave the NICU, the lactation consultant will help you transition from breastfeeding your baby in the NICU to breastfeeding your baby at home.

FIRST WEEK DAILY BREASTFEEDING LOG

Circle the hour when your baby nurses. Put a "B" above the hour of day if your baby nursed both breasts. If one breast only, place "L" for left breast or "R" for right breast. Circle the W when your baby has a wet diaper. Circle the S when your baby has a soiled diaper. It would be best to use cloth diapers or inexpensive disposable diapers the first week of your baby's life. This makes it easier for you to tell if your baby has urinated.

Birthdate:____/____/____   Time:_____ A.M. P.M.

DAY ONE:
Breastfeeding Time:
12 1 2 3 4 5 6 7 8 9 10 11 12 1 2 3 4 5 6 7 8 9 10 11
GOAL: 8 to 12 times per day
Audible swallowing: yes   no
Wet diaper: W
Black tarry soiled diaper: S

DAY TWO:
Breastfeeding Time:
12 1 2 3 4 5 6 7 8 9 10 11 12 1 2 3 4 5 6 7 8 9 10 11
GOAL: 8 to 12 times per day
Audible swallowing: yes   no
Wet diaper: W   W
Black tarry soiled diaper: S   S

DAY THREE:
Breastfeeding Time:

12 1 2 3 4 5 6 7 8 9 10 11 12 1 2 3 4 5 6 7 8 9 10 11

GOAL: 8 to 12 times per day

Audible swallowing: yes   no

Wet diaper: W W W

Green soiled diaper: S S

DAY FOUR:
Breastfeeding Time:

12 1 2 3 4 5 6 7 8 9 10 11 12 1 2 3 4 5 6 7 8 9 10 11

GOAL: 8 to 12 times per day

Audible swallowing: yes   no

Wet diaper: W W W W

Yellow soiled diaper: S S S

DAY FIVE:
Breastfeeding Time:

12 1 2 3 4 5 6 7 8 9 10 11 12 1 2 3 4 5 6 7 8 9 10 11

GOAL: 8 to 12 times per day

Audible swallowing: yes   no

Wet diaper: W W W W

Yellow soiled diaper: S S S

DAY SIX:
Breastfeeding Time:

12 1 2 3 4 5 6 7 8 9 10 11 12 1 2 3 4 5 6 7 8 9 10 11

GOAL: 8 to 12 times per day

Audible swallowing: yes   no

Wet diaper: W W W W

Yellow soiled diaper: S S S S

DAY SEVEN:
Breastfeeding Time:
12 1 2 3 4 5 6 7 8 9 10 11 12 1 2 3 4 5 6 7 8 9 10 11
GOAL: 8 to 12 times per day

Audible swallowing:	yes	no				
Wet diaper:	W	W	W	W	W	W
Yellow soiled diaper:	S	S	S	S		

If your baby is not breastfeeding 8 to 12 times a day or seems to be breastfeeding all the time, or if your baby has fewer wet or soiled diapers than the number on the log, call your baby's health care provider.

What should I do if I
cannot be with my
baby at feeding time?

WHEN YOU ARE AWAY FROM YOUR BABY

EXCLUSIVE BREASTFEEDING for the first 3 to 4 weeks will help establish your milk supply, and it will help your baby develop a strong nursing pattern. The longer you can keep giving your baby only the breast, the easier the nursing "rhythm" between the two of you will be.

But you may be going back to work, or you may want occasional time away from your baby. During these times, your baby can be fed by cup—or by bottle, if you prefer—and you can continue breastfeeding as well. One or two cup-feedings a week may help your baby accept feedings from someone else occasionally. For information about bottlefeeding, see page 45. For information on cup-feeding, consult a lactation specialist, La Leche League, or a care provider. You can also ask the hospital staff to demonstrate this technique after your baby is born.

The best nutrition for your baby comes from your breast milk. Even if you occasionally feed your baby by cup or bottle, it's best to give the baby your expressed breast milk, rather than use prepared formula.

EXPRESSING MILK

You can express milk by hand in this way:
- Circle your breast firmly with your thumb above the nipple and your finger tips below, about an inch and a half back from the nipple.
- Push back toward your chest, then gently squeeze. Have a nurse teach you this in the hospital.

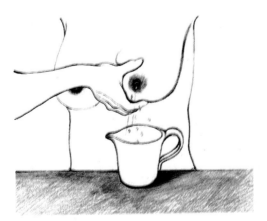

Even if you can't be there for a feeding, you can express and save breast milk for your baby.

There are a variety of breast pumps available, from simple hand-operated pumps to more complex electric machines. If you need to express milk only occasionally, a hand pump probably will do just fine. If you are going back to work, or if you frequently need to be away from your baby, you may wish to rent or buy an electric pump, which allows you to express more milk quickly. (Ask your lactation consultant or care provider about where to buy or rent an effective pump.) Pumps should be clean, durable, comfortable, reliable, easy to use, and not too noisy. Double pumps save time and are most effective at stimulating your milk supply.

If you intend to buy a used pump or share a pump with someone else, contact the manufacturer to make sure it is safe to do so.

STORING MILK

Expressed breast milk can be stored in bottles, plastic bags, or plastic bottle liners. The following chart offers guidelines for freezing and storing breast milk. **Never use a microwave to thaw or warm milk.** Valuable nutrients may be destroyed, and hot spots created in the milk can burn the baby's mouth and throat. Simply set the container of milk in a bowl of hot tap water for a few minutes. Do not refreeze breast milk.

Breast Milk Storage Guidelines

	Room Temperature	Refrigerator	Refrigerator Freezer	Deep Freezer
Freshly Expressed Breast Milk	8 hours	5 days	6 months	12 months
Thawed Breast Milk (previously frozen)	Do not store	24 hours	Never refreeze thawed milk	Never refreeze thawed milk

PACIFIERS

There is some evidence that using a pacifier too soon—or too frequently—can interfere with breastfeeding. To establish a strong milk supply, decrease engorgement, and practice breast-feeding skills, allow the baby to satisfy his or her sucking needs at the breast rather than on a pacifier. If you want to use a paci-fier, wait until the baby is 2 weeks old, and limit his or her use to 30 minutes a day. Or, let the baby suck on your finger instead of a pacifier.

GOING BACK TO WORK

With a little extra planning and organization, it is possible to breastfeed your baby even after you return to work. There are several ways to do this:

- Pump your breast milk at work. Many states require employ-ers to provide time and space for women to pump their breast milk. This allows mothers to provide breast milk for their babies in daycare.
- Instead of pumping your breast milk at work, breastfeed your baby in the morning, evening, and at night. Your ability to keep a strong milk supply may depend on how often you nurse the baby when you are not at work.
- Sleep with your baby, nursing on and off all night to help maintain your milk supply.

It is common for a woman's milk supply to drop when she returns to work. You may want to consider getting a good breast pump and using it several times a day for about two weeks before you go back to work. This will increase your milk supply and compensate for the back-to-work drop-off. You'll also have a stockpile in the freezer for those very busy days.

BREASTFEEDING CONCERNS

SUCCESSFUL BREASTFEEDING means reaching your own goals for nursing your baby, not the goals that others have set for you. Some women experience occasional problems while breastfeeding; however, with the right information and support, most of these problems can be overcome. Be sure to consult a professional lactation consultant, your health care provider, or La Leche League with any questions or concerns you may have. Some of the more common concerns are discussed in the pages that follow.

BABY WON'T LATCH ONTO THE NIPPLE

Newborns don't always latch onto the breast right away to begin nursing. There may be several reasons for this. Babies may be sleepy from a long birth process or from medications that the mother received during labor. Babies may feel sore from the birth or from circumcision. Finally, some mothers have nipples that are flat or inverted, which can make latching difficult.

All of these concerns can be dealt with in the hospital. Parents can also consult a lactation consultant or La Leche League.

LET-DOWN DIFFICULTIES

In the first few days of breastfeeding, you may not feel your milk "letting down" into the breast. Relax, drink fluids, massage your breasts, use warm compresses, or stimulate your nipples to help release the milk. When you hear the baby swallow or you see milk leaking from your other breast, you will know that let-down has occurred. Some women feel a tingling sensation in the breast when the milk is released.

SORE NIPPLES

Sore nipples can be a small irritation, or they can be a very painful problem. Often, sore nipples occur when the baby sucks on the tip of your nipple instead of on most or all of the areola. Here are some suggestions for preventing or minimizing sore nipples:

- **If your breast is engorged or very full, do some gentle massage to express a little milk and soften the breast.** This will help the baby latch onto the breast, and it will start the milk flowing.

What problems might arise during breastfeeding?

- **Tickle the baby's lower lip with your nipple.** This will encourage the baby to open his or her mouth. When the mouth is wide open, put as much of the areola into the baby's mouth as possible, and see that the baby's lips are in the correct "flanged" position (puckered much like a fish).
- **Feed the baby often, starting on the side that is less sore.** Your baby will be less vigorous if he or she is less hungry.
- **Try a new nursing position at each feeding to lessen the pressure on any sore spot.**
- **Do not use soap on your nipples.** Your nipples have special glands that keep them supple and protected. Soap can interfere with this process. Wash your breasts with plain warm water.
- **Rub expressed breast milk over your nipples.** Breast milk has natural healing qualities. You can also use lanolin to lubricate your nipples, if they are sore.
- **If your nipples remain so painful that you don't want to nurse, talk to a lactation consultant or your health care provider as soon as possible.** The earlier you deal with this problem, the easier it will be to correct.

ENGORGEMENT

A few days after your baby is born, fluid and milk can build up in your breasts and make them feel hard, hot, and painful. This is called **engorgement.** Frequent breastfeeding is the best way to prevent engorgement. Other prevention tips include:

- Avoid formula and pacifiers in the early days, and allow the baby to meet his or her sucking needs at the breast as much as possible.
- Massage your breasts to stimulate the let-down of milk.
- If the baby doesn't nurse well, or if your breasts are uncomfortably full after feeding, use a breast pump for 10–15 minutes to relieve the fullness.
- Use ice packs for 15 minutes or so after nursing to help relieve swelling. Limit ice to 15 minutes.
- Consider a pain medication, such as ibuprofen, to help relieve some of the discomfort.

Gently massaging your breast with both hands can help relieve engorgement.

PLUGGED MILK DUCTS AND BREAST INFECTIONS

A plugged milk duct is a temporary lump in the breast that usually occurs on just one side. It can be uncomfortable. Heat, massage, and frequent nursing can help dislodge the plug. If the problem does not resolve in two or three days, call a lactation consultant or your health care provider.

A painful, warm, red area in the breast—along with flu-like symptoms such as chills, achiness, or a temperature over 100.4° F —may indicate a breast infection. If you think you have a breast infection, you need to see your health care provider as quickly as possible. Tell your doctor or nurse practitioner that you are nursing, so he or she can prescribe medications that do not affect breastfeeding. You should also:

- **Empty your breasts completely and frequently.** If the baby can't do this, rent a high-quality, electric, automatic cycling breast pump. You might also have a lactation consultant check to see if the baby is sucking properly.
- **Apply heat and/or cold, and take ibuprofen to reduce pain and inflammation.**
- **Rest in bed with the baby as much as possible, and drink plenty of fluids.**

MILK SUPPLY

Remember, the more your baby nurses, the greater your milk supply will be. Unless your health care provider or lactation consultant recommends it, resist the temptation to feed your baby formula. This can actually decrease your milk supply. Follow these tips:

- **Nurse early and often, rest when you can, eat well, and drink lots of fluids.**
- **If your baby gains weight slowly, reassure yourself by taking the baby to the clinic for frequent weight checks.**
- **Use a high-quality electric double pump to help increase your milk supply.**
- **See pages 33 through 35 to be sure your baby is getting enough milk.**
- **Visit a lactation consultant, who can observe the baby to check for adequate sucking and correct positioning.**

LEAKING BREASTS

Some women find that, once they've been nursing for a week or so, the sound of someone else's baby crying can cause milk to begin leaking from their breasts. This will become less of a problem with time. To handle leaking:

- **Use nursing pads or folded cotton handkerchiefs in your bra, and carry extras.** Avoid pads with plastic liners.
- **If you cannot feed your baby right away, fold your arms across your breasts and press inward on your nipples to stop the leaking.**

BABY REFUSES OR PULLS AWAY FROM THE BREAST

Sometimes, your baby will stop in the middle of a feeding, even though he or she doesn't seem to have taken enough milk. Or, as your baby grows older, he or she may turn away from the breast altogether. There are several reasons why your baby may pull away or refuse the breast:

- **Your baby may have a cold.** A cold can make a baby irritable, and it can make it hard to breathe while nursing. Breastfeeding helps a baby recover sooner.
- **Your baby may need to be burped.** Air in the tummy may make nursing uncomfortable.
- **Milk may come out so quickly that your baby can't swallow it fast enough.** Before nursing, express a little milk to decrease the flow. Or, try feeding in a recliner with the baby lying on top of you. If your baby is gaining weight well, try nursing from one breast per feeding. If the milk flow doesn't improve, talk to a lactation consultant.
- **Your baby may have a yeast infection, called thrush, which makes nursing uncomfortable.** If you see a whitish coating in your baby's mouth that does not wipe off, call your health care provider. Yeast can cause sore nipples and shooting pain in your breasts. If a yeast infection is diagnosed, be sure that both you and your baby are treated. Otherwise, you might pass the infection back and forth to each other.

BOTTLEFEEDING

BREAST MILK is the best food for babies, but prepared infant formulas have been developed to provide nutrition for infants who will be partially breastfed or who will not be breastfed at all.

Babies less than a year old should be fed iron-fortified formula, not regular cow's milk. Talk with your baby's health care provider about what kind of formula to use.

Concentrated liquid or powdered formulas need to be mixed with water. If you live on a city water line, use the water from your sink, so your baby will get enough fluoride and other minerals. If your water is chlorinated, you probably will not need to boil it before use. If you have well water, have the water tested by a certified lab to ensure that it is safe to drink, has enough fluoride, and contains no nitrates. If you choose to mix concentrated liquid or powdered formula with bottled water, find out the source and quality of the water first (much bottled water comes from wells). Like well water, bottled water must contain fluoride—a necessary nutrient—and be free of nitrates. If you use a home water filter, check with the manufacturer to be sure that it doesn't remove the fluoride from the water.

What should I know about formula feeding?

There are several varieties of bottles and nipples available. A regular nipple gives an ample supply of milk and is easy for a baby to suck. Sometimes, however, the flow of milk from these nipples is too fast, and the baby may not be able to keep up. If this happens, try tightening the ring around the nipple to slow the flow. Sometimes finding the "right" nipple is a trial-and-error process, and what's right for your baby may not be right for your sister's baby or your neighbor's baby.

PREPARING FORMULA

- **Use fresh formula.** Don't use formula after the expiration date. Store any opened formula that you don't use in the refrigerator, and throw it away after 48 hours. If the baby leaves formula in his or her bottle after being fed, throw that formula away and wash the bottle thoroughly.
- **Clean bottles thoroughly between feedings.** Use hot, soapy water to wash bottles, nipples, and rings. A bottle brush should be used to scrub the inside of the bottle and the nipple. Rinse everything well.
- **You can give formula at any safe temperature, without worrying about the "right" temperature.** Some babies will drink formula straight from the refrigerator. Others prefer their formula warmed. An easy way to warm formula is simply to hold it under warm running tap water, or to place it in a bowl of warm water for a few minutes. **Never** heat formula in a microwave oven. Test the warmth of the formula on the inside of your wrist before feeding it to the baby.
- **When using concentrated liquid formula:** Clean the top of the can and then shake it before opening. Use a measuring cup and put equal amounts of tap water and liquid formula into a clean bottle, water first. For example, to mix 4 ounces of formula, put 2 ounces of tap water in a bottle, then 2 ounces of concentrated liquid formula. Put a clean nipple on the bottle, then shake to mix the formula and water. Test the temperature of the mixed formula on your wrist to make sure it's not too hot, then feed your baby. Throw away any formula in the bottle you don't use during this feeding.
- **When mixing powdered formula:** Use one scoop of powdered formula (the scoop comes with the formula) for every 2 ounces of tap water. For example, to mix 4 ounces of formula, put 4 ounces of tap water in the bottle, then 2 scoops of powdered formula. Shake well to mix, test the temperature on your wrist, then feed your baby. Again, throw away any formula left in the bottle after the baby eats.

Never try to "stretch" formula, whether liquid or powdered, by adding more water than the directions call for. If you are having trouble finding the money to buy formula, ask your health care provider for information on obtaining assistance through the Women, Infant, and Children (WIC) program administered by the federal government.

FEEDING YOUR BABY A BOTTLE

Always hold your baby while he or she drinks from a bottle. When you're rushed or tired, you may be tempted to prop up a bottle in your baby's mouth so he or she can eat while you do other things. This is a bad idea for you and your baby because:

- **It can be dangerous.** Your baby can choke or develop ear infections.

- **It can cause tooth decay.** The formula (or any other sweet liquid, including breast milk) will pool in your baby's mouth if he or she goes to sleep with a bottle. The natural sugar in the liquid will form an acid that can damage the baby's teeth.

- **It can hurt your baby's emotional development.** Babies need to be touched and held. Feeding is a natural time to cuddle your baby, whether you are breastfeeding or using a bottle. The best thing you can do for your baby is sit quietly in a calm place while feeding your baby.

It's important to hold your baby while you are feeding him or her, whether you are breastfeeding or bottlefeeding.

GETTING STARTED

The log on the following pages will help you keep track of how much formula your baby is taking and whether he or she is having regular wet and soiled diapers.

FIRST WEEK DAILY BOTTLEFEEDING LOG

Circle the hour your baby eats. Circle the W when your baby has a wet diaper. Circle the S when your baby has a soiled diaper. It would be best to use cloth diapers or inexpensive disposable diapers the first week of your baby's life. This makes it easier for you to tell if your baby has urinated.

Birthdate:_____/_____/_____   Time:_____ A.M. P.M.

DAY ONE:
Bottlefeeding Time:
12 1 2 3 4 5 6 7 8 9 10 11 12 1 2 3 4 5 6 7 8 9 10 11
GOAL: 6 to 12 times per day
Audible swallowing: yes   no
Wet diaper: W
Black tarry soiled diaper: S

DAY TWO:
Bottlefeeding Time:
12 1 2 3 4 5 6 7 8 9 10 11 12 1 2 3 4 5 6 7 8 9 10 11
GOAL: 6 to 12 times per day
Audible swallowing: yes   no
Wet diaper: W   W
Black tarry soiled diaper: S   S

DAY THREE:
Bottlefeeding Time:
12 1 2 3 4 5 6 7 8 9 10 11 12 1 2 3 4 5 6 7 8 9 10 11
GOAL: 6 to 12 times per day
Audible swallowing: yes   no
Wet diaper: W   W   W
Green soiled diaper: S   S

Day Four:

Bottlefeeding Time:

12 1 2 3 4 5 6 7 8 9 10 11 12 1 2 3 4 5 6 7 8 9 10 11

GOAL: 6 to 12 times per day

Audible swallowing: yes no

Wet diaper: W   W   W   W

Yellow soiled diaper: S   S

Day Five:

Bottlefeeding Time:

12 1 2 3 4 5 6 7 8 9 10 11 12 1 2 3 4 5 6 7 8 9 10 11

GOAL: 6 to 12 times per day

Audible swallowing: yes no

Wet diaper: W   W   W   W

Yellow soiled diaper: S   S   S

Day Six:

Bottlefeeding Time:

12 1 2 3 4 5 6 7 8 9 10 11 12 1 2 3 4 5 6 7 8 9 10 11

GOAL: 6 to 12 times per day

Audible swallowing: yes no

Wet diaper: W   W   W   W

Yellow soiled diaper: S   S   S

Day Seven:

Bottlefeeding Time:

12 1 2 3 4 5 6 7 8 9 10 11 12 1 2 3 4 5 6 7 8 9 10 11

GOAL: 6 to 12 times per day

Audible swallowing: yes no

Wet diaper: W   W   W   W   W   W

Yellow soiled diaper: S   S   S

If your baby is not eating 6 to 12 times a day or seems to be eating all the time, or if your baby has fewer wet or soiled diapers than the number on the log, call your baby's health care provider.

FOR PARTNERS

IF THE BABY'S mother is breastfeeding, you may think there's not much you can do now. For some partners, this is a relief; for others, it feels like they're missing out on something special.

Be sure to attend a breastfeeding class with your partner. You will be better able to support her if you are well informed about infant feeding. While it's true you can't nurse the baby, you can help your partner nurse, and you can take part in that special bonding experience. You can be the one to pick up the crying baby in the middle of the night, change his or her diaper, and bring the baby to the mother for nursing. This helps the nursing mother get a little more sleep. You can also rock, hold, or burp the baby after feeding. Or, you might simply rejoice in the wonder of it all. Let your partner know how proud you are of her, and support her in caring for the baby.

You may be a bit jealous, or upset, by seeing your partner's breasts in a completely different way than you're used to. Or you may be somewhat aroused. These are all normal feelings. It may help to talk about them with your partner or someone else.

FOR MORE INFORMATION

Nursing Mother, Working Mother by Gayle Pryor.
The Nursing Mother's Companion by Kathleen Huggins, et al.
The Womanly Art of Breastfeeding by La Leche League.

Breastfeeding.com <www.breastfeeding.com>.
La Leche League <www.lalecheleague.org>, 1-847-519-7730.
Medela, Inc. <www.medela.com>, 1-800-435-8316.
Hollister, Inc. <www.hollister.com>, 1-800-323-4060.

Your Baby's First 15 Months

You wondered what your baby would be like, and now the baby is here, a separate person who needs a lot from you.

The first 15 months of your baby's life are important for physical, mental, and emotional development. You want to take care of your baby the best way you can, whether that means getting the proper immunizations or playing games that will help your baby's development.

The first 15 months will be a busy time as your baby changes from a helpless newborn to a little person who walks and talks and shows you an independent personality.

SOME OF THE QUESTIONS ANSWERED
IN THIS CHAPTER INCLUDE:

- What makes a good parent?
- What changes will I see in my baby?
- How do I keep my baby safe?
- How can I help my baby develop?
- What immunizations will my baby need?
- When will my baby start eating solid food?
- When will my baby start to walk?

BECOMING A PARENT

A THREE-YEAR-OLD girl is told that her mommy is going to have a new baby and that she "is going to be a big sister." She looks forward to it for months. Then the new baby is born and the three-year-old is very upset. "You said I was going to be a *big* sister," she cries. "But I'm still the same size!"

When you have your first baby, you may feel a lot like that three-year-old. Now you have a baby, but you're still the same person. What does it take to be a *parent?*

We have to learn how to be parents the same way we learn most things: by getting information, by watching others, by doing.

What makes a good parent?

- **Getting information.** While you were pregnant, you may have read books about pregnancy, childbirth, and babies. There are dozens of books about children and parenting available (see the list of resources at the end of this chapter, for example). Numerous videos and audiotapes are also available. In most communities there are groups devoted to supporting and educating parents. One such group is La Leche League, which has chapters everywhere in the United States. It not only helps new mothers breastfeed, but also offers opportunities for sharing parenting information and concerns with other mothers. Check with your health care provider for information about this and other groups in your community.

- **Watching others.** The example for raising children that has probably had the most influence on you is that set by your own parents. But now that you have your own baby, you need to stop and think about what kind of parents you had and what parts of their parenting style you want to keep—and what parts you don't.

    Your mother may have been wonderful at changing your diapers and keeping you fed and clean, but perhaps she was uncomfortable showing emotion, so she didn't kiss or hug you often. Or she may have been affectionate and warm, but missed appointments at the clinic and rarely cooked a meal.

Think about your friends and other relatives. What do you see about the way they raise their children that you like? What do you see that you don't like? Whose children seem happy and loved? Don't be afraid to ask others about their ideas on being a parent, and don't be afraid to ignore any ideas that don't seem right to you.

Decide what your priorities are—and what's best for your child. No parent is perfect, but we all want to be the best parent we can be.

- **Doing.** No matter how much you've read about being a parent or watched other parents, you will learn most about how to be a parent simply by *being* one.

If you don't know how to change a diaper, the nurses at the hospital will teach you before you go home. But you will only become good at changing diapers after you've changed a few by yourself.

If you're nervous about breastfeeding, your health care provider, a nurse, or a lactation specialist will help you get started. But it's only by doing it that you will find the positions that work best for you and your baby.

Because you will pay attention to your own child, you will learn the difference between your baby's tired cry and your baby's hungry cry. You will learn that your child is uneasy around other people and needs to be held when visitors are around—or you'll learn that your child loves the attention of other people and may need a little control in order not to become too excited.

SPIRITUAL CONCERNS

As a new parent, you will face a number of spiritual questions: What does it mean to love? What is self-sacrifice? How do you balance parenthood with other aspects of your life? Take the time to think about these questions and discuss them with other parents, your family, your friends, and your partner. As you face the spiritual joys and struggles of parenting, you will learn profound lessons about who you are and how you live out your beliefs.

THE MOST IMPORTANT PERSON IN YOUR BABY'S LIFE IS YOU

A child's first important connection is with his or her parents. It's a connection that starts even before the baby is born. Recent studies show that babies can hear while they are still in the womb, and that they remember what they hear in some way. Since the sound they will hear most often is the mother's voice, a newborn baby responds more to the mother's voice than to the voice of anyone else.

In some cultures, babies are strapped to their mothers' backs or chests for most of the day and night during the first months after birth. This practice is uncommon in the United States, but American babies still need to sense the warmth, sounds, and smells of the mother. The more you hold your baby and talk to your baby and play with your baby, the better.

Being a parent is not a part-time job. It's a lot of hard work—and it's a lot of fun. There is nothing that can make you happier than watching your baby's face when you walk into a room.

Even if you work outside the home, you are still a full-time parent. Other people may take care of your baby while you're at work, but you are still the most important person in your baby's life. Although you may be tired when you get home, you need to make sure your child doesn't miss your attention. Now is the time to pick up your baby or toddler, cuddle, sing a song, or read a story. Show your love. It's a good way for you to relax after work, and it's something your baby needs.

PARENTING PROBLEMS

If you feel overwhelmed, tell someone. Your health care provider can help direct you to services or counselors when you think you just can't handle your child or being a parent. Being a parent *is* hard, even when everything is fine. If you have a colicky baby who cries all the time, or a toddler who seems out of control, parenting can seem impossible.

Don't be embarrassed to admit that you don't think you can handle the situation. Most parents have felt that way at one time or another. Sometimes a little reassurance is all you need to feel more confident.

Whatever you do, *never* take your frustration out on your child. If you feel in danger of losing control, get help immediately. Find someone to look after your child for an hour or two while you do what you need to calm down, whether that involves taking a nap, walking around the block, or talking to a friend or relative.

It is especially important that you never shake your baby. Shaking can cause permanent brain damage, even death. Make it clear to your daycare providers and babysitters that they should never shake your baby either, for any reason. Ask them to call you to pick up your baby if they feel that they're "losing control."

You and your baby share a special connection. Spend time looking into your baby's face, talking, and showing different expressions.

YOUR BABY: 2 WEEKS TO 2 MONTHS

DURING THE FIRST 2 months of your baby's life, you will see big changes in the way your baby looks, acts, and even "talks" to you. From a newborn who doesn't seem to do much more than eat, sleep, and cry, your baby will grow very quickly into a little person who smiles and coos and examines the world.

NUTRITION

- The only food your baby needs right now is breast milk or iron-fortified formula. Do not try to introduce any other foods when your baby is this young; the baby's digestive system is not ready to handle them.
- You will be feeding your baby every 2 to 4 hours, although the schedule is likely to change from day to day.
- The more often your baby eats during the day, the more likely the baby is to sleep for a longer stretch (5 to 8 hours) at night.

ELIMINATION

- Breastfed babies usually have small, seedy, yellowish or golden stools—and they have them fairly often, especially for the first 7 weeks. As the baby gets older, there should be fewer stools each day.
- Babies that are fed formula have 1 to 4 stools a day. These stools should be soft, and the color will vary depending on the type of formula used.
- You will learn to recognize your baby's normal stools. Watch for any big change in the color, frequency, or texture of your baby's stools. It can be a sign of allergy (to formula or to something you may have eaten that is passed on through breast milk) or of illness.
- Your baby should have 6 to 8 wet diapers every day, with small amounts of urine each time.

SLEEP

- Babies at this age sleep from 16 to 20 hours a day. Your baby's sleep pattern will vary from day to day.
- If your baby sleeps longer than 3½ to 4 hours during the day, wake the baby for a feeding. You want to save the longer sleep periods for night, when you can sleep, too.

- When you feed your baby at night, do it with a little more peace and quiet than during the day, so the baby will go back to sleep rather than think it's playtime.
- Babies should be put to sleep on their backs or sides, *not* on their tummies. Tummy-sleeping has been found to be associated with Sudden Infant Death Syndrome (SIDS).
- You can have your baby sleep in a separate room, in bed with you, or in a cradle or crib in your bedroom. If you decide to let your baby sleep in a crib, review the safety measures described on page 16.
- A bedtime routine will help your baby learn when to sleep as he or she grows. The routine might include washing the baby with a washcloth, putting on a fresh diaper and clean clothes, feeding and burping the baby, then rocking or sitting together in a quiet, dimly-lit room until the baby falls asleep.

GROWTH AND DEVELOPMENT

- Your baby can hear from the moment of birth. The baby may react to sounds by blinking, crying, getting quiet, or startling (a jerky motion). Your baby knows the sound of your voice at birth and will keep learning and responding to your voice.
- A newborn can see about a foot away. By the time your baby is 2 months old, he or she will be able to see things about 10 feet away. At about 6 weeks old, your baby should start to follow things—especially you—with his or her eyes and to smile back at you when you are smiling.
- At about 2 to 3 weeks, your baby may begin to have a period of crying, usually in the early evening. This is a normal fussy period, but it is sometimes hard on parents because it may seem like nothing you do helps calm your baby. Try to soothe your baby by rocking, walking, or patting him or her on the back. You might want to wrap the baby snuggly in a blanket or try feeding him or her again. It is not recommended that you allow your baby to "cry it out" at this age. Keep this up until the crying stops—the entire process can

What changes will I see in my baby?

take as long as 2 to 3 hours. Babies eventually outgrow this fussiness.

- **Colic** is an extended period of crying, usually in the evening hours. Babies with colic appear to be in pain, and parents are often unable to soothe them. Use the calming techniques listed on page 15, and keep the baby close in a front-pack carrier or sling. Try to go about your routine as much as possible. If you are very concerned, call your health care provider. This can be a stressful time for parents.

SOCIAL

- As the baby develops, he or she will begin to smile at people, usually parents, brothers and sisters, daycare providers, and others who are around often and are part of the baby's life.
- By the time your baby is 2 months old, he or she will show excitement—moving arms and legs, making noises, smiling—and will be able to calm himself or herself by sucking on fingers or a pacifier.
- Your baby will show that he or she likes to be with people, staying awake longer when people are around and even "showing off" for others.

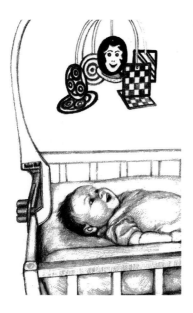

Mobiles and other bright objects or pictures may attract your baby's attention and interest.

How do I keep my
baby safe?

How can I help my
baby develop?

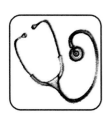

What immunizations
will my baby need?

SAFETY

- Always use an approved car seat, and place it facing the rear, preferably in the middle of the back seat.
- Never leave your baby alone on a high place or in bath water, not even for a quick moment. Babies can roll off a dressing table or sink under the water in seconds.
- Always hold your baby when feeding a bottle. Leaving a bottle propped up so your baby can feed without you being there can cause choking, and it has been found to increase ear infections.

ACTIVITIES TO HELP YOUR BABY'S DEVELOPMENT

- Put your baby on his or her stomach on a flat surface. Talk, show toys, or hold up a mirror to encourage your baby to try to lift his or her head, thereby strengthening the shoulder and neck muscles. (Don't leave your baby on his or her stomach to fall asleep.)
- Hold your baby in a sitting position in your lap, facing you. Hold your baby's shoulders forward, giving more support. From this position, your baby can see what's going on around him or her and can look into your eyes.
- Put your baby on his or her back and encourage arm and foot movement by putting brightly colored or noise-making toys on a foot or hand.

CLINIC VISITS

After your first clinic visit with your new baby, your health care provider will establish a schedule for health exams. The times you see the health care provider are usually planned to coincide with the schedule for immunizations.

You may see your health care provider during your baby's first 2 months if your baby is ill with a cold or ear infection. The tiny body of your baby can get very sick quickly, so don't wait to talk with your health care provider if your baby seems sick.

The immunizations given during the first 2 months are:

- **Hepatitis B.** This prevents infection of the liver that can be caused by the hepatitis B virus. The first shot of this vaccine is usually given between 2 weeks and 2 months, and the second shot between 2 months and 4 months.

- **DTP or DTAP.** This combination immunization protects against diphtheria, pertussis (whooping cough), and tetanus. The first shot is given at 2 months.
- **Polio.** The polio vaccine can be given as either an oral solution or an injection. Polio can paralyze or kill, but because of the vaccine, it is far less common today than it was forty to fifty years ago.
- **Hib.** This vaccine protects against the Haemophilus influenzae type B bacteria, which can cause brain damage, pneumonia, infection, and even death in young children. The vaccine is given in a shot, starting at 2 months.

At your baby's 2-month clinic visit, he or she will get 3 or 4 immunizations, depending on the current medical recommendations. Most babies cry when they get shots, but their discomfort is very brief.

Non-Prescription Pain and Fever Medication

Your baby is likely to get a number of colds and viruses during his or her first 15 months, and your health care provider may recommend that you give your baby an over-the-counter medication like Tylenol or Advil to help control the fever and ease his or her aches and pains. (You should not give medications, especially aspirin, to your baby without the advice of your health care provider.) The chart below shows the correct dosages for your baby as he or she grows and gains weight.

	ACETAMINOPHEN (Tylenol, Tempra)		IBUPROFEN (Motrin, Advil, Pediaprofen)	
WEIGHT IN POUNDS	INFANT DROPS 80 mg/0.8 ml	ELIXIR/SUSPENSION 160 mg/5 ml	INFANT DROPS 50 mg/1.25 ml	Suspension 100 mg/5 ml
12–14	0.8 ml	1/2 tsp	1.25 ml	1/2 tsp
15–17	1.0 ml	2/3 tsp	2.0 ml	3/4 tsp
18–22	1.2 ml	3/4 tsp	2.5 ml	1 tsp
23–29	1.6 ml	1 tsp	3.25 ml	1 1/4 tsp
30–34	2.0 ml	1 1/4 tsp	3.75 ml	1 1/2 tsp
35–40	2.4 ml	1 1/2 tsp	–	1 3/4 tsp
41–46	–	1 3/4 tsp	–	2 tsp
47–52	–	2 tsp	–	2 1/2 tsp

A few times a day, put your baby on his or her tummy and show toys or other inter-esting things. This will encourage your baby to lift his or her head and strengthen the neck and spine.

YOUR BABY: 2 MONTHS TO 4 MONTHS

THIS CAN BE an easy-going time. Your baby cries less—the early-evening fussy period usually disappears by 3 months—and sleeps more. Your baby is more interested in the world and in other people, and is easier to take places with you. Routines are becoming established, with more regular times for eating, sleeping, and playing.

Your tiredness and feelings of frustration are likely to be over as well. When you look at this happy little baby who smiles every time you come into the room, you forget that there may have been some difficult times during the first 2 months.

NUTRITION

- Breast milk or iron-fortified formula is still the best nourishment for your baby, and other foods should not be introduced yet. If you think your baby needs cereal or other solids, talk about it with your health care provider before you feed them to your baby.
- Your baby will breastfeed about 6 times a day.
- If you are feeding your baby formula, he or she should take 20 to 32 ounces of formula a day.
- Your baby will take most feedings during the day and sleep longer at night.

ELIMINATION

- Breastfed babies may have stools several times a day or as seldom as once a week. Either, or any number in between, is normal if it is a regular pattern for your baby.
- Formula-fed babies usually have from 1 stool every few days to 4 a day. These stools are soft.
- Most infants urinate often, in small amounts. Your baby should have several wet diapers each day.

SLEEP

- Most babies begin to sleep longer at night—7 to 8 hours. They may then wake up for a feeding and fall back asleep for another 3 to 4 hours. (Which means you get more sleep now, too.)

- Naps during the day can vary. Your baby may take one short nap, one long nap, or none at all. Or your baby may take several naps.
- You can help your baby learn how to go to sleep on his or her own now. When you notice your baby getting tired, try putting him or her in the crib while still awake, so he or she can learn how to go from being awake to being asleep.
- Give the last feeding about half an hour to an hour before putting your baby into the crib for the night, so your baby learns to separate the idea of eating from sleeping.

What changes will I see in my baby?

GROWTH AND DEVELOPMENT

- Your baby's vision is now like that of an adult, and the eye adjusts to objects at different distances.
- Your baby will play with his or her fingers.
- Your baby begins to reach for and grab things, although still clumsily. Your baby may be able to bear weight on his or her feet, and to lift the chest up when placed on his or her tummy.
- Drooling starts at about 3 months, although teething doesn't usually start until 6 to 10 months.
- Your baby learns by putting things in his or her mouth, starting with his or her own fingers and then anything else in reach.

SOCIAL

- Your baby smiles, coos, and responds to people—especially you. By the fourth month, your baby may be able to have a whole "conversation," babbling and cooing sounds in a string. In a good mood, your baby may squeal, giggle, laugh, and grin for as long as 30 minutes.
- If people are around to socialize with your baby, he or she will play twice as long as when alone.

SAFETY

- Keep using the rear-facing car seat in the back seat of your car.
- Do not leave your baby alone in a high place or in the bath. Your baby is getting more active and can flip off a table, bed, or countertop very quickly.
- Don't eat or drink hot items while holding your baby. Your baby is starting to grab at things and could get a bad burn.

How do I keep my baby safe?

ACTIVITIES TO HELP YOUR BABY'S DEVELOPMENT

- A few times a day, put your baby on his or her tummy when awake. This will help muscles develop, and your baby will learn to roll over.
- Let your baby play without any clothes on sometimes. A good place is on a towel in the middle of a double bed, with you right there. At 2 to 3 months, a baby likes being naked. Since the baby learns about the world largely through touching things, being naked lets your baby feel different textures. Being without clothes also lets the baby find his or her own body parts.
- Your baby likes looking at new things—and putting them into the mouth. Toys or objects of varying color, weight, and texture will stimulate your baby. You don't need anything fancy, but make sure that whatever your baby is playing with is safe.
- Hold your baby so he or she can see your face, and talk gently. When your baby responds in some way, answer back, as if you are having a real conversation.
- Continue to read, tell stories, and talk to your baby. Such activities can have dramatic effects on future learning.

How can I help my baby develop?

CLINIC VISITS

The second immunizations for diphtheria-tetanus-pertussis, polio, and Hib are usually given at 4 months. If the first hepatitis B vaccine was given at 2 months, the second will be given at 3 or 4 months.

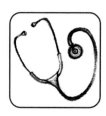

What immunizations will my baby need?

YOUR BABY: 4 MONTHS TO 6 MONTHS

YOUR BABY starts to get very active during these 2 months, learning to control more muscles, exploring the world more actively—and putting everything into the mouth.

When will my baby start eating solid food?

NUTRITION

- Breast milk or iron-fortified formula will give all of the nourishment your baby needs, but you may see signs that your baby is ready to try solid foods.
- Signs that your baby is ready for solid foods include:
  - suddenly taking more formula or nursing more
  - waking up hungry in the middle of the night
  - seeming to want to eat when others—you or other adults or children—are eating.
- A good first solid food is rice or oatmeal cereal. Start with about a tablespoon of dry cereal mixed with water, breast milk, formula, or non-citrus fruit juice (*not* orange juice) diluted with an equal amount of water.
- Some babies like their cereal thick, some like it thin. Experiment to see what your baby prefers.
- Between 4 to 8 tablespoons of dry cereal in one or two meals is a day's serving.
- After your baby has been eating cereal for a week or two, you can begin to try feeding pureed fruits and vegetables. Only do this if your baby seems to want more solids.
- Your baby should be nursing 4 to 6 times a day, or taking 20 to 35 ounces of formula a day.

ELIMINATION

- As your baby starts to eat solid foods, stools will change. If your baby has firmer stools, use oatmeal rather than rice cereal.
- Your baby's bladder is growing, and your baby won't need to urinate quite as often. You will not have to change diapers as often now, but they should be wetter when you do change them.
- All of your baby's feedings should be during the day now.

SLEEP

- Most babies now sleep about 10 hours through the night.
- If you haven't started a sleep routine for your baby, do it now. When your baby begins to look tired at night, get him or her ready for bed and put the baby in the crib while his or her eyes are open, so your baby can become familiar and comfortable with being in the crib and falling to sleep. Once your baby can go to sleep at the beginning of the night, he or she will be able to go back to sleep if wakened in the middle of the night.
- Naps vary. On average, your baby will take 3 naps during the day.

GROWTH AND DEVELOPMENT

- Your baby doesn't want to miss a minute of the world right now and may fuss when you put him or her on the tummy because it's harder to see.
- Most babies will learn to roll from front to back, and from back to front, during these months.
- Starting at about 3 months, babies need time to play independently, as well as to play with others.
- Your baby's reach is getting better, and everything will go into the mouth.
- With support, your baby can sit for a half hour or more.

What changes will I see in my baby?

SOCIAL

- Your baby is very social now and enjoys seeing new places and new people. It's a good time to use babysitters, if you haven't already, because your baby is more likely to accept the occasional care of another person.
- Your baby is able to play alone now and needs some time to do that so he or she knows how to be alone.

SAFETY

- Keep using the rear-facing child seat in your car if your baby weighs less than 20 pounds dressed.
- Don't leave your baby alone in high places or in the bath.
- Start childproofing your house—your baby will be mobile soon. Go around your house at baby level and see what your baby will soon be able to get into. Are there uncovered outlets?

How can I keep my
baby safe?

Electric cords to pull? Breakable items just inside cabinet doors? Heavy things that can be pulled or pushed over? Cleaning supplies, insecticides, drain cleaners, or other poisonous materials? For the next few years, you will need to adapt your home for the safety of your baby. Get dangerous items or materials out of reach—or out of the house altogether.

- Feed your baby solid food when he or she is strapped in a sturdy infant seat or chair.
- Be careful handling hot items around your baby; his or her hands are very quick to grab things now.
- Although your baby can use a walker, they are not recommended. It's too easy for a baby to roll one right down a flight of stairs.

ACTIVITIES TO HELP YOUR BABY'S DEVELOPMENT

- Lots of tummy time on the floor will help your baby develop upper-body strength and learn to roll over. Your baby may fuss, though, when placed on the tummy.
- Jump-ups are fine for short periods, as long as your baby is not standing on his or her toes too much.
- Spend time looking into your baby's face and talking to him or her. Your baby will make sounds to try to keep your attention. Smile and talk as if you were having a conversation.

How can I help my
baby develop?

- Give your baby safe objects and toys to grab, mouth, and shake. Show your baby different things to look at, from flowers in your garden to pictures on the wall.
- Your baby might be very interested in the sounds and images on television right now, but it's not good for your baby to spend too much time in front of the television. Infants need to be with real people who can respond to their needs and behaviors, not unresponsive images of people on a TV set.
- Reading simple infant books to your child continues to be instrumental to his or her intellectual development.

CLINIC VISITS

At 6 months, your baby will have another DTP and Hib vaccination. Depending on the schedule used, a third polio immunization and hepatitis B vaccination may be given now also.

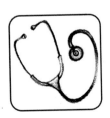

Babies 4 to 6 months old enjoy grabbing and mouthing things. Give your baby a variety of safe objects to explore. After 6 months, even if your baby is not ready to walk, he or she will try to pull to a standing position to get a new view of the world.

YOUR BABY: 6 MONTHS TO 10 MONTHS

YOUR BABY is learning to control his or her body and is becoming much more independent. From rolling over to crawling—even walking. From sucking on a finger to grabbing anything in reach. From the first smile and coo to a real word. All of these things are possible during these months.

Babies develop in different ways and at somewhat different rates. Your baby may be walking by 9 months—or barely crawling. Talk with your health care provider about how your baby is developing.

NUTRITION

- Solids are becoming as important as breast milk or formula. By 8 to 12 months, most babies are getting most of their nutrition through solid foods.
- When your baby can sit in a highchair and seems interested in what other people in the family are eating, you can start feeding soft table foods rather than pureed baby foods.
- A good choice for your baby's first finger food is 1/4 of a graham cracker. It's easy to hold, and it dissolves quickly as the baby gums it.
- If your baby seems to gag on graham crackers or other soft table foods, wait a couple of weeks and then try again. Sometimes a baby just isn't interested yet, or the new texture is too strange. Some babies like new textures; others need to try something several times before they accept it.
- It's best to stick to a few new foods every few days so you don't overwhelm your baby.
- At about 7 or 8 months, try feeding your baby a regular Cheerio. If your baby can pick it up and eat it successfully, he or she is ready to try all soft table foods.
- A food is safe for your baby if it is about the size of a Cheerio and can be squeezed between your forefinger and thumb.
- By 9 to 10 months, your baby will be nursing 2 or 3 times a day or taking 16 to 24 ounces of formula.

ELIMINATION

- Stools continue to vary, depending on what you are feeding your baby. They are likely to have a stronger smell now, more like adult stools.
- It is not unusual to have a few stools per day some days, and none on others.

SLEEP

- Night routines are usually established and your baby should sleep 10 to 12 hours without waking.
- Nap patterns are now more regular, timed with meals. Two to three naps a day are common.
- Your baby will average about 14 hours of sleep a day.
- Between 6 and 12 months, your baby may wake at night. Give your baby a chance to go back to sleep without help.
- When your baby starts to grow teeth, gently brush them with plain water or wipe them with a cloth as part of the bedtime routine. This will help your child develop good toothbrushing habits as he or she grows.

GROWTH AND DEVELOPMENT

- Your baby will begin to sit without help, pull to a stand, crawl, and maybe even walk. The average age to walk is 12½ months.
- Your baby may begin saying some simple words around 8 to 10 months. "Mama," "dada," "bye-bye," and, of course, "no." At first these words will seem almost like accidents, but by 10 to 15 months, your baby probably will know how to use the simple words correctly.
- As your baby gets more active and more involved with the world, it's common for some fears to appear. A baby who always loved being bathed may develop a fear of water. A very sociable baby now only wants to be held by Mom. A baby who was eating solid foods pushes them away.

When will my baby start to walk?

What changes will I see in my baby?

SOCIAL

- Your baby likes to play with you and others. Children this age like to watch other children play. If you have older children, they are likely to be your baby's favorite entertainment now.
- Boys begin to identify with men and older boys, girls with women and older girls.
- Your baby will have different moods and will be more sensitive to the moods of other people. If you are upset, your baby is going to know it—and probably will get upset, too.
- Your baby's personality is getting stronger all the time. He or she likes some things and not others. There may be a favorite toy, a favorite game, a favorite story, a favorite piece of music.
- As your baby learns more about the world, you need to teach what is okay and what is not. Instead of saying "no" all the time, try to give your baby something else to do or hold or play with. Set limits now on what your baby can do and what your baby can't do. For example, don't let your baby play with remote controls, telephones, or other things that are not toys and that you don't want your baby to play with in the future. If your baby grabs one of these items, give an acceptable toy or object instead and take away the wrong one.

SAFETY

- When your baby weighs 20 pounds in clothing, you can switch to a front-facing child seat in the car. The middle of the back seat is still the safest seating position.
- Put the mattress in your baby's crib at the lowest position, once your baby can get into a sitting position without help.
- Put the phone number for your local poison control center in a place where it is easy to see and use. Buy a bottle of ipecac and use only under the direction of the poison control center to make your baby vomit potentially poisonous substances.
- Once your baby can sit alone, try to avoid lightweight chairs or carriages that may tip over as your baby moves or shifts weight.

How do I keep my baby safe?

ACTIVITIES TO HELP YOUR BABY'S DEVELOPMENT

- Talk to your baby, face to face. Use simple words over and over, like your baby's name or a food or a special toy. Talk to your baby while you do things together. If you take your baby grocery shopping, talk about what foods you see on the shelf. Ask your baby to point to the peas, or the milk. Then point to it yourself.

- If you haven't been reading to your baby already, now is an important time to start. Even very small babies recognize the pictures and then the stories of their favorite books. Babies and small children like to hear the same story over and over again. That's how they learn to connect the words and the pictures to the story.

- Be dramatic. When you talk and play with your baby, use lots of different expressions, tones of voice, and movements of your hands and body.

- Give your baby room to move. A carpeted playroom floor is perfect, but not every family has that. In order to experiment with movements like rolling over, crawling, and walking, your baby needs a space without a lot of furniture or other things that can be tipped over or broken.

- Let your baby watch you do things. Babies at this age like to watch people do normal activities, like cooking, housework, and gardening. Find a safe thing your baby can do while you work. Give your baby a spoon to bang or a safe piece of food to play with while you cook. Let your baby crawl in the grass while you garden.

How can I help my baby develop?

CLINIC VISITS

Depending on your clinic's schedule, your baby may have a checkup between 9 and 12 months. Some clinics do the third hepatitis B shot and may also check your baby's iron level, or hemoglobin, by taking a small sample of blood from your baby's finger.

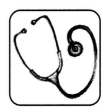

Exploring the outdoors is exciting for your toddler. Even on cold days, bundle up your baby and spend some time outside.

YOUR BABY: 10 MONTHS TO 15 MONTHS

YOUR BABY is becoming a toddler now, walking, eating solid foods, talking, and becoming more independent. Sometimes this can be hard, for you and your baby. Your baby has plenty of strong likes and dislikes and can be very stubborn. But your baby needs you to set limits and to keep him or her safe. There are a lot of struggles between parents and children at this stage. Remember: you're the adult. You need to protect your child even as you let him or her know that it is okay to do some things independently.

NUTRITION

- By about a year old, most babies eat all soft table foods and want to feed themselves.
- Your baby can start using a cup now. You should try to have your baby off bottles by 12 to 15 months.
- If your baby is eating from all of the major food groups, you can replace formula with whole cow's milk.
- Your baby should eat mostly grains, such as cereal, bread, pasta, and rice, followed by fruits and vegetables and high-protein foods such as dairy products and meats. By a year old, 12 to 18 ounces of milk a day is enough.
- Small servings will encourage your baby to eat; you can always give more if your baby is still hungry.
- The correct servings for children this age are: a half-piece of bread, waffle, or bagel; 1/4 to 1/2 cup of cereal or pasta; one tablespoon of fruit, vegetable, or meat; 6 ounces of milk; 4 ounces of yogurt; 1 ounce or 1 slice of cheese.
- Using child-sized dishes, spoons, and forks helps your baby learn table skills. He or she will watch others to see how to use utensils.

ELIMINATION

- Stools and urine are usually predictable by now, although stools may change in frequency or consistency when new foods are introduced.

Sleep

- Your baby may be so active that you will need to start a cooling-down period before bedtime, with quiet play to calm your baby.
- Naps should be consistent, usually 2 of them a day.
- Your baby will sleep about 15 hours a day.
- Clean your baby's teeth with water before bedtime.

Growth and Development

- Nearly all babies begin walking at this age.
- Your baby can use hands and fingers to grasp, throw, and drop things.
- Your baby understands many words and can follow simple commands.
- Babies are able to use at least simple words, and some babies will be able to talk quite a bit by 15 months. You should let your baby know that you are happy to hear his or her words.

Social

- Your baby's moods and preferences are obvious now, and sometimes a problem. Since your baby can also use the word "no," you may feel like you are in a struggle for control.
- Your baby is very sensitive to approval from others, especially you. While letting your baby know what he or she can do and what is not allowed, always show that you love your baby.
- "Separation anxiety" may show up, even with a baby who has been used to seeing lots of different people. You can help your baby understand that you will come back by practicing short separations and then coming back. Don't drag good-byes out when you leave your baby in daycare or with a babysitter; it only makes your baby more anxious. Say good-bye lovingly but firmly, then leave in a positive way.
- Teaching right from wrong is your main job as a parent now. Decide what is acceptable and what is not. You and others in the family should be united in how you deal with unacceptable behavior. If you don't want your baby to throw food, but your husband and older child simply laugh, your baby is going to be confused about what the rules are.

SAFETY

- Make sure your house is child-proofed, with gates on stairs, plugs in outlets, and latches on cabinet doors. Keep breakable items out of reach.
- Use a child-safety seat in your car at all times.
- Never leave your child alone near water.

ACTIVITIES TO HELP YOUR BABY'S DEVELOPMENT

- Give your baby a play space somewhere near where you usually are. A playroom in another part of the house is not as good as a space in the living room, next to where you are reading or cleaning.
- Let your baby explore the outdoors. Even in cold climates, a baby can be bundled up and taken outside to feel the snow or scuff through piles of fallen leaves. In good weather, there are hundreds of sights and sounds and things to feel.

How can I help my baby develop?

- Talk to your child as you do things together. If you are cooking dinner, describe what you're doing in simple terms. If you are getting ready to give your baby a bath, list each body part as it is washed: "Now we wash your hand, now we wash your elbow, now we wash your shoulder. . . ."
- Let your baby regularly play around other children of the same age. Although a child this young doesn't really play with others, he or she will learn a lot from watching other children and will get used to being with others. If your child is in daycare with other children, this is already a part of his or her life. But if your child is home with you and you have no other children, try to find an informal group of parents with other toddlers, or sign up for a parent-child class.

CLINIC VISITS

Between 12 and 18 months, your child will get a DTAP and a Hib booster. During this same time, measles-mumps-rubella (MMR) and chicken pox vaccinations will be given. These last two immunizations protect your child from some dangerous illnesses that used to be common in childhood. An oral polio and a hepatitis B shot may be given, depending on your clinic's immunization schedule.

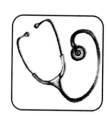

FOR PARTNERS

BABIES FORM special relationships with all people who care for them. The more loving people there are in their lives, the better off they will be.

Almost everything the baby's mother can do with the baby now can also be done by you. You can share the bathing and diapering and rocking. As the baby grows, you can share feeding.

Most important, you can share in activities that help the baby grow and develop. Talk to the baby, play with the baby, hold the baby.

When your baby is old enough to get around independently, you and your partner should agree on what kind of limits you want in your house, and then keep those limits consistent.

You and your partner need to spend time alone together. Sometimes that seems impossible with a small baby in the house. And sometimes mothers are reluctant to leave their babies even for a short time. You can encourage your partner to get out, with you and on her own, for some quality "adult" time. If you arrange for the child care, you can help make that evening out a reality.

FOR MORE INFORMATION

Games to Play with Babies by Jackie Silberg.
Taking Care of Your Child by Robert H. Pantell, MD, et al.
Your Baby and Child: From Birth to Age Five by Penelope Leach.
The New First Three Years of Life by Burton L. White.
The Magic Years by Selma Fraiberg.
How to Get Your Kid to Eat . . . But Not Too Much by E. Satter.
The First Twelve Months of Life by Frank and Theresa Caplan.

American Academy of Pediatrics <www.aap.org>.
Buckle Up Kids <www.buckleupkids.state.mn.us>.
Fathering Magazine <www.fathermag.com>.
Fathers.com <www.fathers.com>.
Parenthood.com <www.parenthood.com>.
Parent Soup <www.parentsoup.com>.
ParentsPlace.com <www.parentsplace.com>.

Keeping Track of Your Baby

You may have a baby album to keep track of photographs and special moments in your baby's life, but these pages can help you work with your health care provider and give you a space to log a few of your baby's important developments.

YOU AND YOUR HEALTH CARE PROVIDER
QUESTIONS YOU HAVE ABOUT YOUR BABY'S DEVELOPMENT

When you think of something you want to remember to ask your health care provider, write it here. Take this book with you each time your baby goes to the clinic.

WHAT YOUR BABY IS DOING

It helps your health care provider if you keep track of your baby's regular eating, sleeping, and waking patterns:

How much does your baby sleep each day? When? What is the longest time your baby sleeps?

_____

_____

How much does your baby nurse (or take bottles) every day?

_____

_____

What kind of stools does your baby have? How often?

_____

_____

How much does your baby cry? What kind of crying?

_____

_____

How much of the day is your baby alert?

_____

_____

Use this space to jot down anything that you think you might need to talk about.

_____

_____

_____

_____

_____

CLINIC VISITS

Use this space to record each well-baby visit to your health care provider.

Date of visit

_____

Baby's height or length   Baby's weight

_____

Immunizations

_____

Comments by health care provider about your baby's development

_____

_____

_____

_____

Date of visit

_____

Baby's height or length   Baby's weight

_____

Immunizations

_____

Comments by health care provider about your baby's development

_____

_____

_____

_____

Date of visit

_____

Baby's height or length   Baby's weight

_____

Immunizations

_____

_____

Comments by health care provider about your baby's development

_____

_____

_____

_____

Date of visit

_____

Baby's height or length   Baby's weight

_____

Immunizations

_____

_____

Comments by health care provider about your baby's development

_____

_____

_____

_____

Date of visit

_____

Baby's height or length   Baby's weight

_____

Immunizations

_____

_____

Comments by health care provider about your baby's development

_____

_____

_____

_____

Date of visit

_____

Baby's height or length   Baby's weight

_____

Immunizations

_____

_____

Comments by health care provider about your baby's development

_____

_____

_____

_____

Date of visit

_____

Baby's height or length   Baby's weight

_____

Immunizations

_____

_____

Comments by health care provider about your baby's development

_____

_____

_____

_____

Date of visit

_____

Baby's height or length   Baby's weight

_____

Immunizations

_____

_____

Comments by health care provider about your baby's development

_____

_____

_____

_____

Date of visit

_____

Baby's height or length   Baby's weight

_____

Immunizations

_____

Comments by health care provider about your baby's development

_____

_____

_____

_____

Date of visit

_____

Baby's height or length   Baby's weight

_____

Immunizations

_____

Comments by health care provider about your baby's development

_____

_____

_____

_____

BABY'S FIRSTS
USE THIS SPACE to record some of the important—or fun—first times in your baby's life.

FIRST SMILE

Date
_____

Smiled at . . .
_____

Occasion
_____

FIRST ROLLED OVER

Date
_____

Occasion
_____

FIRST LAUGHED

Date
_____

Laughed at . . .
_____

Occasion
_____

FIRST HAIRCUT

Date
_____

FIRST SAT UP

Date
_____

FIRST STEPS ALONE

Date

FIRST FAVORITE TOY

What was the toy?

When did it become a favorite?

FIRST WORD

Date

To whom?

What was the word?

FIRST FRIEND

Name

How did they become friends?

What have they done together?

FIRST COMPLETE SENTENCE

Date

What was it?

Occasion

OTHER IMPORTANT FIRSTS

Index